Gymnastics Journal

My Scores, My Goals, My Dreams

Karen Goeller, CSCS

GymnasticsBooks.com   © 2013 Goeller

Gymnastics Journal
My Scores, My Goals, My Dreams
Karen Goeller, CSCS

Copyright © 2013 Goeller
All Rights Reserved.
Gymnastics Stuff, NJ

No part of this book may be reproduced in whole or in part in any form or by any means, electronic or mechanical including photocopying, recording, or by any information storage and retrieval system now known or hereafter invented without written permission from the author and publisher. The Gymnastics Stuff and Strength Teacher Logos are the property of Gymnastics Stuff and may not be used or reproduced without the express written permission of Gymnastics Stuff. Most of Karen Goeller's books are available at quantity discounts. For information please write to the author and publisher. Contact information can be found through the website, GymnasticsBooks.com.

ISBN-13: 978-1489583437
ISBN-10: 1489583432

Gymnastics Journal: My Scores, My Goals, My Dreams

Congratulations on making the decision to keep track of your scores, goals, thoughts, and dreams.

Whether you are just beginning to compete or you've been competing for several years, keeping a journal is a great way to set goals and preserve memories.

Years from now this journal may be picked up and the reader will be brought back in time.

Maybe the goals will be reached or maybe they will be changed, but at the very least the gymnast using this journal will have preserved gymnastics moments and memories.

Gymnastics Journal: My Scores, My Goals, My Dreams

Gymnastics Journal: My Scores, My Goals, My Dreams

Gymnastics Journal: My Scores, My Goals, My Dreams

Gymnastics Journal: My Scores, My Goals, My Dreams

Gymnastics Journal: My Scores, My Goals, My Dreams

Gymnastics Journal: My Scores, My Goals, My Dreams

Gymnastics Journal: My Scores, My Goals, My Dreams

Gymnastics Journal: My Scores, My Goals, My Dreams

Date of Meet
Name of Meet
Location of Meet
Level Competing Today
My Teammates Today

My Coach Today
How am I going to relax today?

Am I ready to focus?

Main Goal for Meet

Event & Score Goals for Today
Beam
Bars
Floor
Vault
All Around

Scores Today
| Vault | Bars | Beam | Floor | AA |

Did I meet my score goals?
What mistakes did I make today?

Will I do anything differently next meet?

GymnasticsBooks.com © 2013 Goeller

Gymnastics Journal: My Scores, My Goals, My Dreams

Main Goal for Next Meet

Event & Score Goals for Next Meet
Beam
Bars
Floor
Vault
All Around

One Month Goals

End of Season Goals

One Year Goals

My Dreams

My Thoughts

Gymnastics Journal: My Scores, My Goals, My Dreams

Gymnastics Journal: My Scores, My Goals, My Dreams

Gymnastics Journal: My Scores, My Goals, My Dreams

Date of Meet _____
Name of Meet _____
Location of Meet _____
Level Competing Today _____
My Teammates Today _____
_____
_____

My Coach Today _____
How am I going to relax today? _____
_____

Am I ready to focus? _____
_____

Main Goal for Meet _____
_____
_____

Event & Score Goals for Today
Beam _____
Bars _____
Floor _____
Vault _____
All Around _____

Scores Today
Vault	Bars	Beam	Floor	AA

Did I meet my score goals? _____
What mistakes did I make today? _____
_____

Will I do anything differently next meet? _____
_____

GymnasticsBooks.com © 2013 Goeller

Gymnastics Journal: My Scores, My Goals, My Dreams

Main Goal for Next Meet
_____
_____

Event & Score Goals for Next Meet
Beam _____
Bars _____
Floor _____
Vault _____
All Around _____

One Month Goals
_____
_____
_____

End of Season Goals
_____
_____

One Year Goals
_____
_____
_____
_____

My Dreams
_____
_____
_____
_____

My Thoughts
_____
_____
_____

Gymnastics Journal: My Scores, My Goals, My Dreams

Gymnastics Journal: My Scores, My Goals, My Dreams

Gymnastics Journal: My Scores, My Goals, My Dreams

Date of Meet _____
Name of Meet _____
Location of Meet _____
Level Competing Today _____
My Teammates Today _____
_____

My Coach Today _____
How am I going to relax today? _____
_____

Am I ready to focus? _____

Main Goal for Meet _____
_____
_____

Event & Score Goals for Today _____
Beam _____
Bars _____
Floor _____
Vault _____
All Around _____

Scores Today _____

Vault	Bars	Beam	Floor	AA

Did I meet my score goals? _____
What mistakes did I make today? _____
_____

Will I do anything differently next meet? _____
_____

GymnasticsBooks.com   © 2013 Goeller

Gymnastics Journal: My Scores, My Goals, My Dreams

Main Goal for Next Meet

Event & Score Goals for Next Meet
Beam
Bars
Floor
Vault
All Around

One Month Goals

End of Season Goals

One Year Goals

My Dreams

My Thoughts

Gymnastics Journal: My Scores, My Goals, My Dreams

Gymnastics Journal: My Scores, My Goals, My Dreams

Gymnastics Journal: My Scores, My Goals, My Dreams

Date of Meet _____
Name of Meet _____
Location of Meet _____
Level Competing Today _____
My Teammates Today _____
_____
_____

My Coach Today _____
How am I going to relax today? _____
_____

Am I ready to focus? _____

Main Goal for Meet _____
_____
_____

Event & Score Goals for Today
Beam _____
Bars _____
Floor _____
Vault _____
All Around _____

Scores Today

Vault	Bars	Beam	Floor	AA

Did I meet my score goals? _____
What mistakes did I make today? _____

Will I do anything differently next meet? _____
_____

GymnasticsBooks.com © 2013 Goeller

Gymnastics Journal: My Scores, My Goals, My Dreams

Main Goal for Next Meet
_____
_____

Event & Score Goals for Next Meet
Beam _____
Bars _____
Floor _____
Vault _____
All Around _____

One Month Goals
_____
_____
_____

End of Season Goals
_____
_____

One Year Goals
_____
_____
_____
_____

My Dreams
_____
_____
_____

My Thoughts
_____
_____
_____

Gymnastics Journal: My Scores, My Goals, My Dreams

Gymnastics Journal: My Scores, My Goals, My Dreams

Gymnastics Journal: My Scores, My Goals, My Dreams

Date of Meet _____

Name of Meet _____

Location of Meet _____

Level Competing Today _____

My Teammates Today _____

_____

_____

My Coach Today _____

How am I going to relax today? _____

_____

Am I ready to focus? _____

_____

Main Goal for Meet _____

_____

_____

Event & Score Goals for Today

Beam _____

Bars _____

Floor _____

Vault _____

All Around _____

Scores Today

Vault	Bars	Beam	Floor	AA

Did I meet my score goals? _____

What mistakes did I make today? _____

_____

Will I do anything differently next meet? _____

_____

GymnasticsBooks.com   © 2013 Goeller

Gymnastics Journal: My Scores, My Goals, My Dreams

Main Goal for Next Meet
_____
_____

Event & Score Goals for Next Meet
Beam _____
Bars _____
Floor _____
Vault _____
All Around _____

One Month Goals
_____
_____
_____

End of Season Goals
_____
_____

One Year Goals
_____
_____
_____
_____

My Dreams
_____
_____
_____
_____

My Thoughts
_____
_____
_____

Gymnastics Journal: My Scores, My Goals, My Dreams

Gymnastics Journal: My Scores, My Goals, My Dreams

Gymnastics Journal: My Scores, My Goals, My Dreams

Date of Meet _____
Name of Meet _____
Location of Meet _____
Level Competing Today _____
My Teammates Today _____
_____

My Coach Today _____
How am I going to relax today? _____
_____

Am I ready to focus? _____

Main Goal for Meet _____
_____
_____

Event & Score Goals for Today _____
Beam _____
Bars _____
Floor _____
Vault _____
All Around _____

Scores Today _____

Vault	Bars	Beam	Floor	AA

Did I meet my score goals? _____
What mistakes did I make today? _____
_____
Will I do anything differently next meet? _____
_____

GymnasticsBooks.com © 2013 Goeller

Gymnastics Journal: My Scores, My Goals, My Dreams

Main Goal for Next Meet
_____
_____

Event & Score Goals for Next Meet
Beam _____
Bars _____
Floor _____
Vault _____
All Around _____

One Month Goals
_____
_____
_____

End of Season Goals
_____
_____

One Year Goals
_____
_____
_____
_____

My Dreams
_____
_____
_____

My Thoughts
_____
_____
_____

Gymnastics Journal: My Scores, My Goals, My Dreams

GymnasticsBooks.com © 2013 Goeller

Gymnastics Journal: My Scores, My Goals, My Dreams

Gymnastics Journal: My Scores, My Goals, My Dreams

Date of Meet
Name of Meet
Location of Meet
Level Competing Today
My Teammates Today

My Coach Today
How am I going to relax today?

Am I ready to focus?

Main Goal for Meet

Event & Score Goals for Today
Beam
Bars
Floor
Vault
All Around

Scores Today
Vault   Bars   Beam   Floor   AA

Did I meet my score goals?
What mistakes did I make today?

Will I do anything differently next meet?

GymnasticsBooks.com   © 2013 Goeller

Gymnastics Journal: My Scores, My Goals, My Dreams

Main Goal for Next Meet
_____
_____
_____

Event & Score Goals for Next Meet
Beam _____
Bars _____
Floor _____
Vault _____
All Around _____

One Month Goals
_____
_____
_____

End of Season Goals
_____
_____

One Year Goals
_____
_____
_____
_____

My Dreams
_____
_____
_____
_____

My Thoughts
_____
_____
_____

Gymnastics Journal: My Scores, My Goals, My Dreams

Gymnastics Journal: My Scores, My Goals, My Dreams

Gymnastics Journal: My Scores, My Goals, My Dreams

Date of Meet _____
Name of Meet _____
Location of Meet _____
Level Competing Today _____
My Teammates Today _____
_____

My Coach Today _____
How am I going to relax today? _____
_____
Am I ready to focus? _____
_____
Main Goal for Meet _____
_____
_____

Event & Score Goals for Today
Beam _____
Bars _____
Floor _____
Vault _____
All Around _____

Scores Today
Vault	Bars	Beam	Floor	AA

Did I meet my score goals? _____
What mistakes did I make today? _____
_____
Will I do anything differently next meet? _____
_____

Gymnastics Journal: My Scores, My Goals, My Dreams

Main Goal for Next Meet
_____
_____

Event & Score Goals for Next Meet
Beam _____
Bars _____
Floor _____
Vault _____
All Around _____

One Month Goals
_____
_____
_____

End of Season Goals
_____
_____

One Year Goals
_____
_____
_____
_____

My Dreams
_____
_____
_____
_____

My Thoughts
_____
_____
_____

Gymnastics Journal: My Scores, My Goals, My Dreams

Gymnastics Journal: My Scores, My Goals, My Dreams

Gymnastics Journal: My Scores, My Goals, My Dreams

Date of Meet _____
Name of Meet _____
Location of Meet _____
Level Competing Today _____
My Teammates Today _____
_____
_____

My Coach Today _____
How am I going to relax today? _____
_____

Am I ready to focus? _____

Main Goal for Meet _____
_____
_____

Event & Score Goals for Today _____
Beam _____
Bars _____
Floor _____
Vault _____
All Around _____

Scores Today

Vault	Bars	Beam	Floor	AA

Did I meet my score goals? _____
What mistakes did I make today? _____
_____

Will I do anything differently next meet? _____
_____

GymnasticsBooks.com © 2013 Goeller

Gymnastics Journal: My Scores, My Goals, My Dreams

Main Goal for Next Meet
_____
_____

Event & Score Goals for Next Meet
Beam _____
Bars _____
Floor _____
Vault _____
All Around _____

One Month Goals
_____
_____
_____

End of Season Goals
_____

One Year Goals
_____
_____
_____
_____

My Dreams
_____
_____
_____

My Thoughts
_____
_____
_____

Gymnastics Journal: My Scores, My Goals, My Dreams

Gymnastics Journal: My Scores, My Goals, My Dreams

Gymnastics Journal: My Scores, My Goals, My Dreams

Date of Meet _____
Name of Meet _____
Location of Meet _____
Level Competing Today _____
My Teammates Today _____
_____

My Coach Today _____
How am I going to relax today? _____
_____

Am I ready to focus? _____

Main Goal for Meet _____
_____
_____

Event & Score Goals for Today
Beam _____
Bars _____
Floor _____
Vault _____
All Around _____

Scores Today

Vault	Bars	Beam	Floor	AA

Did I meet my score goals? _____
What mistakes did I make today? _____

Will I do anything differently next meet? _____
_____

GymnasticsBooks.com © 2013 Goeller

Gymnastics Journal: My Scores, My Goals, My Dreams

Main Goal for Next Meet

_____
_____

Event & Score Goals for Next Meet

Beam _____
Bars _____
Floor _____
Vault _____
All Around _____

One Month Goals

_____
_____

End of Season Goals

_____
_____

One Year Goals

_____
_____
_____
_____

My Dreams

_____
_____
_____
_____

My Thoughts

_____
_____
_____

GymnasticsBooks.com   © 2013 Goeller

Gymnastics Journal: My Scores, My Goals, My Dreams

GymnasticsBooks.com © 2013 Goeller

Gymnastics Journal: My Scores, My Goals, My Dreams

Gymnastics Journal: My Scores, My Goals, My Dreams

Date of Meet _____
Name of Meet _____
Location of Meet _____
Level Competing Today _____
My Teammates Today _____
_____
_____

My Coach Today _____
How am I going to relax today? _____
_____

Am I ready to focus? _____

Main Goal for Meet _____
_____
_____

Event & Score Goals for Today
Beam _____
Bars _____
Floor _____
Vault _____
All Around _____

Scores Today
Vault	Bars	Beam	Floor	AA

Did I meet my score goals? _____
What mistakes did I make today? _____
_____
Will I do anything differently next meet? _____
_____

GymnasticsBooks.com © 2013 Goeller

Gymnastics Journal: My Scores, My Goals, My Dreams

Main Goal for Next Meet
_____
_____

Event & Score Goals for Next Meet
Beam _____
Bars _____
Floor _____
Vault _____
All Around _____

One Month Goals
_____
_____
_____

End of Season Goals
_____
_____
_____

One Year Goals
_____
_____
_____
_____

My Dreams
_____
_____
_____
_____

My Thoughts
_____
_____
_____

Gymnastics Journal: My Scores, My Goals, My Dreams

Gymnastics Journal: My Scores, My Goals, My Dreams

Gymnastics Journal: My Scores, My Goals, My Dreams

Date of Meet _____
Name of Meet _____
Location of Meet _____
Level Competing Today _____
My Teammates Today _____
_____
_____

My Coach Today _____
How am I going to relax today? _____
_____

Am I ready to focus? _____
_____

Main Goal for Meet _____
_____
_____
_____

Event & Score Goals for Today _____
Beam _____
Bars _____
Floor _____
Vault _____
All Around _____

Scores Today

Vault	Bars	Beam	Floor	AA

Did I meet my score goals? _____
What mistakes did I make today? _____
_____
Will I do anything differently next meet? _____
_____

GymnasticsBooks.com © 2013 Goeller

Gymnastics Journal: My Scores, My Goals, My Dreams

Main Goal for Next Meet
_____
_____

Event & Score Goals for Next Meet
Beam _____
Bars _____
Floor _____
Vault _____
All Around _____

One Month Goals
_____
_____
_____

End of Season Goals
_____
_____

One Year Goals
_____
_____
_____
_____

My Dreams
_____
_____
_____
_____

My Thoughts
_____
_____
_____

GymnasticsBooks.com © 2013 Goeller

Gymnastics Journal: My Scores, My Goals, My Dreams

Gymnastics Journal: My Scores, My Goals, My Dreams

GymnasticsBooks.com © 2013 Goeller

Gymnastics Journal: My Scores, My Goals, My Dreams

Date of Meet
Name of Meet
Location of Meet
Level Competing Today
My Teammates Today

My Coach Today
How am I going to relax today?

Am I ready to focus?

Main Goal for Meet

Event & Score Goals for Today
Beam
Bars
Floor
Vault
All Around

Scores Today
| Vault | Bars | Beam | Floor | AA |

Did I meet my score goals?
What mistakes did I make today?

Will I do anything differently next meet?

GymnasticsBooks.com © 2013 Goeller

Gymnastics Journal: My Scores, My Goals, My Dreams

Main Goal for Next Meet
_____
_____
_____

Event & Score Goals for Next Meet
Beam _____
Bars _____
Floor _____
Vault _____
All Around _____

One Month Goals
_____
_____
_____

End of Season Goals
_____
_____

One Year Goals
_____
_____
_____
_____

My Dreams
_____
_____
_____
_____

My Thoughts
_____
_____
_____

Gymnastics Journal: My Scores, My Goals, My Dreams

Gymnastics Journal: My Scores, My Goals, My Dreams

Gymnastics Journal: My Scores, My Goals, My Dreams

Date of Meet _____
Name of Meet _____
Location of Meet _____
Level Competing Today _____
My Teammates Today _____
_____

My Coach Today _____
How am I going to relax today? _____
_____

Am I ready to focus? _____

Main Goal for Meet _____
_____
_____

Event & Score Goals for Today
Beam _____
Bars _____
Floor _____
Vault _____
All Around _____

Scores Today
Vault	Bars	Beam	Floor	AA

Did I meet my score goals? _____
What mistakes did I make today? _____
_____
Will I do anything differently next meet? _____
_____

GymnasticsBooks.com © 2013 Goeller

Gymnastics Journal: My Scores, My Goals, My Dreams

Main Goal for Next Meet
_____
_____

Event & Score Goals for Next Meet
Beam _____
Bars _____
Floor _____
Vault _____
All Around _____

One Month Goals
_____
_____
_____

End of Season Goals
_____
_____

One Year Goals
_____
_____
_____
_____

My Dreams
_____
_____
_____

My Thoughts
_____
_____
_____

GymnasticsBooks.com © 2013 Goeller

Gymnastics Journal: My Scores, My Goals, My Dreams

Gymnastics Journal: My Scores, My Goals, My Dreams

Gymnastics Journal: My Scores, My Goals, My Dreams

Date of Meet _____
Name of Meet _____
Location of Meet _____
Level Competing Today _____
My Teammates Today _____
_____
_____

My Coach Today _____
How am I going to relax today? _____
_____

Am I ready to focus? _____
_____

Main Goal for Meet _____
_____
_____

Event & Score Goals for Today
Beam _____
Bars _____
Floor _____
Vault _____
All Around _____

Scores Today

Vault	Bars	Beam	Floor	AA

Did I meet my score goals? _____
What mistakes did I make today? _____
_____
Will I do anything differently next meet? _____
_____

GymnasticsBooks.com © 2013 Goeller

Gymnastics Journal: My Scores, My Goals, My Dreams

Main Goal for Next Meet
_____
_____
_____

Event & Score Goals for Next Meet
Beam _____
Bars _____
Floor _____
Vault _____
All Around _____

One Month Goals
_____
_____
_____

End of Season Goals
_____
_____

One Year Goals
_____
_____
_____
_____

My Dreams
_____
_____
_____
_____

My Thoughts
_____
_____
_____
_____

Gymnastics Journal: My Scores, My Goals, My Dreams

Gymnastics Journal: My Scores, My Goals, My Dreams

Gymnastics Journal: My Scores, My Goals, My Dreams

Date of Meet _____
Name of Meet _____
Location of Meet _____
Level Competing Today _____
My Teammates Today _____
_____
_____

My Coach Today _____
How am I going to relax today? _____
_____

Am I ready to focus? _____

Main Goal for Meet _____
_____
_____

Event & Score Goals for Today

Beam	
Bars	
Floor	
Vault	
All Around	

Scores Today

Vault	Bars	Beam	Floor	AA

Did I meet my score goals? _____
What mistakes did I make today? _____
_____

Will I do anything differently next meet? _____
_____

Gymnastics Journal: My Scores, My Goals, My Dreams

Main Goal for Next Meet
_____
_____

Event & Score Goals for Next Meet
Beam _____
Bars _____
Floor _____
Vault _____
All Around _____

One Month Goals
_____
_____

End of Season Goals
_____
_____

One Year Goals
_____
_____
_____
_____

My Dreams
_____
_____
_____
_____

My Thoughts
_____
_____
_____

GymnasticsBooks.com © 2013 Goeller

Gymnastics Journal: My Scores, My Goals, My Dreams

GymnasticsBooks.com © 2013 Goeller

Gymnastics Journal: My Scores, My Goals, My Dreams

Gymnastics Journal: My Scores, My Goals, My Dreams

Date of Meet _____
Name of Meet _____
Location of Meet _____
Level Competing Today _____
My Teammates Today _____
_____

My Coach Today _____
How am I going to relax today? _____
_____

Am I ready to focus? _____

Main Goal for Meet _____
_____
_____

Event & Score Goals for Today _____
Beam _____
Bars _____
Floor _____
Vault _____
All Around _____

Scores Today

Vault	Bars	Beam	Floor	AA

Did I meet my score goals? _____
What mistakes did I make today? _____
_____
Will I do anything differently next meet? _____
_____

GymnasticsBooks.com © 2013 Goeller

Gymnastics Journal: My Scores, My Goals, My Dreams

Main Goal for Next Meet
_____
_____
_____

Event & Score Goals for Next Meet
Beam _____
Bars _____
Floor _____
Vault _____
All Around _____

One Month Goals
_____
_____
_____

End of Season Goals
_____
_____

One Year Goals
_____
_____
_____
_____
_____

My Dreams
_____
_____
_____
_____

My Thoughts
_____
_____
_____
_____

Gymnastics Journal: My Scores, My Goals, My Dreams

Gymnastics Journal: My Scores, My Goals, My Dreams

Gymnastics Journal: My Scores, My Goals, My Dreams

<u>Date of Meet</u>
<u>Name of Meet</u>
<u>Location of Meet</u>
<u>Level Competing Today</u>
<u>My Teammates Today</u>

<u>My Coach Today</u>
<u>How am I going to relax today?</u>

<u>Am I ready to focus?</u>

<u>Main Goal for Meet</u>

<u>Event & Score Goals for Today</u>
<u>Beam</u>
<u>Bars</u>
<u>Floor</u>
<u>Vault</u>
<u>All Around</u>

<u>Scores Today</u>

Vault	Bars	Beam	Floor	AA

<u>Did I meet my score goals?</u>
<u>What mistakes did I make today?</u>

<u>Will I do anything differently next meet?</u>

GymnasticsBooks.com © 2013 Goeller

Gymnastics Journal: My Scores, My Goals, My Dreams

Main Goal for Next Meet
_____
_____

Event & Score Goals for Next Meet
Beam _____
Bars _____
Floor _____
Vault _____
All Around _____

One Month Goals
_____
_____

End of Season Goals
_____
_____

One Year Goals
_____
_____
_____
_____

My Dreams
_____
_____
_____
_____

My Thoughts
_____
_____
_____
_____

GymnasticsBooks.com © 2013 Goeller

Gymnastics Journal: My Scores, My Goals, My Dreams

Gymnastics Journal: My Scores, My Goals, My Dreams

Gymnastics Journal: My Scores, My Goals, My Dreams

Date of Meet
Name of Meet
Location of Meet
Level Competing Today
My Teammates Today

My Coach Today
How am I going to relax today?

Am I ready to focus?

Main Goal for Meet

Event & Score Goals for Today
Beam
Bars
Floor
Vault
All Around

Scores Today

Vault	Bars	Beam	Floor	AA

Did I meet my score goals?
What mistakes did I make today?

Will I do anything differently next meet?

GymnasticsBooks.com © 2013 Goeller

Gymnastics Journal: My Scores, My Goals, My Dreams

Main Goal for Next Meet
_____
_____

Event & Score Goals for Next Meet
Beam _____
Bars _____
Floor _____
Vault _____
All Around _____

One Month Goals
_____
_____

End of Season Goals
_____
_____

One Year Goals
_____
_____
_____
_____

My Dreams
_____
_____
_____
_____

My Thoughts
_____
_____
_____

GymnasticsBooks.com © 2013 Goeller

Gymnastics Journal: My Scores, My Goals, My Dreams

Gymnastics Journal: My Scores, My Goals, My Dreams

Gymnastics Journal: My Scores, My Goals, My Dreams

Date of Meet
Name of Meet
Location of Meet
Level Competing Today
My Teammates Today

My Coach Today
How am I going to relax today?

Am I ready to focus?

Main Goal for Meet

Event & Score Goals for Today
Beam
Bars
Floor
Vault
All Around

Scores Today
Vault	Bars	Beam	Floor	AA

Did I meet my score goals?
What mistakes did I make today?

Will I do anything differently next meet?

GymnasticsBooks.com © 2013 Goeller

Gymnastics Journal: My Scores, My Goals, My Dreams

Main Goal for Next Meet
_____
_____

Event & Score Goals for Next Meet
Beam _____
Bars _____
Floor _____
Vault _____
All Around _____

One Month Goals
_____
_____

End of Season Goals
_____
_____

One Year Goals
_____
_____
_____
_____

My Dreams
_____
_____
_____
_____

My Thoughts
_____
_____
_____
_____

Gymnastics Journal: My Scores, My Goals, My Dreams

Gymnastics Journal: My Scores, My Goals, My Dreams

Gymnastics Journal: My Scores, My Goals, My Dreams

Date of Meet _____
Name of Meet _____
Location of Meet _____
Level Competing Today _____
My Teammates Today _____
_____

My Coach Today _____
How am I going to relax today? _____
_____

Am I ready to focus? _____
_____

Main Goal for Meet _____
_____
_____

Event & Score Goals for Today
Beam _____
Bars _____
Floor _____
Vault _____
All Around _____

Scores Today
Vault	Bars	Beam	Floor	AA

Did I meet my score goals? _____
What mistakes did I make today? _____
_____

Will I do anything differently next meet? _____
_____

GymnasticsBooks.com © 2013 Goeller

Gymnastics Journal: My Scores, My Goals, My Dreams

Main Goal for Next Meet
_____
_____

Event & Score Goals for Next Meet
Beam _____
Bars _____
Floor _____
Vault _____
All Around _____

One Month Goals
_____
_____

End of Season Goals
_____
_____

One Year Goals
_____
_____
_____
_____

My Dreams
_____
_____
_____
_____

My Thoughts
_____
_____
_____

Gymnastics Journal: My Scores, My Goals, My Dreams

Gymnastics Journal: My Scores, My Goals, My Dreams

Gymnastics Journal: My Scores, My Goals, My Dreams

Date of Meet _____
Name of Meet _____
Location of Meet _____
Level Competing Today _____
My Teammates Today _____
_____
_____

My Coach Today _____
How am I going to relax today? _____
_____

Am I ready to focus? _____
_____

Main Goal for Meet _____
_____
_____

Event & Score Goals for Today _____
Beam _____
Bars _____
Floor _____
Vault _____
All Around _____

Scores Today

Vault	Bars	Beam	Floor	AA

Did I meet my score goals? _____
What mistakes did I make today? _____
_____
Will I do anything differently next meet? _____
_____

GymnasticsBooks.com   © 2013 Goeller

Gymnastics Journal: My Scores, My Goals, My Dreams

Main Goal for Next Meet
_____
_____

Event & Score Goals for Next Meet
Beam _____
Bars _____
Floor _____
Vault _____
All Around _____

One Month Goals
_____
_____

End of Season Goals
_____
_____

One Year Goals
_____
_____
_____
_____

My Dreams
_____
_____
_____
_____

My Thoughts
_____
_____
_____
_____

GymnasticsBooks.com   © 2013 Goeller

Gymnastics Journal: My Scores, My Goals, My Dreams

Gymnastics Journal: My Scores, My Goals, My Dreams

GymnasticsBooks.com © 2013 Goeller

Gymnastics Journal: My Scores, My Goals, My Dreams

Date of Meet

Name of Meet

Location of Meet

Level Competing Today

My Teammates Today

My Coach Today

How am I going to relax today?

Am I ready to focus?

Main Goal for Meet

Event & Score Goals for Today
Beam
Bars
Floor
Vault
All Around

Scores Today
Vault	Bars	Beam	Floor	AA

Did I meet my score goals?
What mistakes did I make today?

Will I do anything differently next meet?

GymnasticsBooks.com   © 2013 Goeller

Gymnastics Journal: My Scores, My Goals, My Dreams

Main Goal for Next Meet
_____
_____

Event & Score Goals for Next Meet
Beam _____
Bars _____
Floor _____
Vault _____
All Around _____

One Month Goals
_____
_____
_____

End of Season Goals
_____
_____

One Year Goals
_____
_____
_____
_____
_____

My Dreams
_____
_____
_____
_____

My Thoughts
_____
_____
_____
_____

GymnasticsBooks.com   © 2013 Goeller

Gymnastics Journal: My Scores, My Goals, My Dreams

Gymnastics Journal: My Scores, My Goals, My Dreams

Gymnastics Journal: My Scores, My Goals, My Dreams

Date of Meet _____

Name of Meet _____

Location of Meet _____

Level Competing Today _____

My Teammates Today _____
_____
_____

My Coach Today _____

How am I going to relax today? _____
_____

Am I ready to focus? _____

Main Goal for Meet _____
_____
_____

Event & Score Goals for Today

Beam	
Bars	
Floor	
Vault	
All Around	

Scores Today

Vault	Bars	Beam	Floor	AA

Did I meet my score goals? _____

What mistakes did I make today? _____
_____

Will I do anything differently next meet? _____
_____

GymnasticsBooks.com © 2013 Goeller

Gymnastics Journal: My Scores, My Goals, My Dreams

Main Goal for Next Meet
_____
_____

Event & Score Goals for Next Meet
Beam _____
Bars _____
Floor _____
Vault _____
All Around _____

One Month Goals
_____
_____
_____

End of Season Goals
_____
_____

One Year Goals
_____
_____
_____
_____

My Dreams
_____
_____
_____
_____

My Thoughts
_____
_____
_____

GymnasticsBooks.com © 2013 Goeller

Gymnastics Journal: My Scores, My Goals, My Dreams

Gymnastics Journal: My Scores, My Goals, My Dreams

Gymnastics Journal: My Scores, My Goals, My Dreams

Date of Meet _____
Name of Meet _____
Location of Meet _____
Level Competing Today _____
My Teammates Today _____
_____
_____

My Coach Today _____
How am I going to relax today? _____
_____

Am I ready to focus? _____
_____

Main Goal for Meet _____
_____
_____

Event & Score Goals for Today
Beam _____
Bars _____
Floor _____
Vault _____
All Around _____

Scores Today

Vault	Bars	Beam	Floor	AA

Did I meet my score goals? _____
What mistakes did I make today? _____
_____

Will I do anything differently next meet? __
_____

GymnasticsBooks.com   © 2013 Goeller

Gymnastics Journal: My Scores, My Goals, My Dreams

Main Goal for Next Meet
_____
_____

Event & Score Goals for Next Meet
Beam _____
Bars _____
Floor _____
Vault _____
All Around _____

One Month Goals
_____
_____
_____

End of Season Goals
_____
_____

One Year Goals
_____
_____
_____
_____

My Dreams
_____
_____
_____
_____

My Thoughts
_____
_____
_____
_____

Gymnastics Journal: My Scores, My Goals, My Dreams

GymnasticsBooks.com © 2013 Goeller

Gymnastics Journal: My Scores, My Goals, My Dreams

Gymnastics Journal: My Scores, My Goals, My Dreams

Date of Meet _____

Name of Meet _____

Location of Meet _____

Level Competing Today _____

My Teammates Today _____

_____

_____

My Coach Today _____

How am I going to relax today? _____

_____

Am I ready to focus? _____

Main Goal for Meet _____

_____

_____

Event & Score Goals for Today _____

Beam _____

Bars _____

Floor _____

Vault _____

All Around _____

Scores Today _____

Vault	Bars	Beam	Floor	AA

Did I meet my score goals? _____

What mistakes did I make today? _____

_____

Will I do anything differently next meet? _____

_____

GymnasticsBooks.com   © 2013 Goeller

Gymnastics Journal: My Scores, My Goals, My Dreams

Main Goal for Next Meet
_____
_____

Event & Score Goals for Next Meet
Beam _____
Bars _____
Floor _____
Vault _____
All Around _____

One Month Goals
_____
_____

End of Season Goals
_____
_____

One Year Goals
_____
_____
_____
_____

My Dreams
_____
_____
_____
_____

My Thoughts
_____
_____
_____
_____

Gymnastics Journal: My Scores, My Goals, My Dreams

Gymnastics Journal: My Scores, My Goals, My Dreams

Gymnastics Journal: My Scores, My Goals, My Dreams

Date of Meet
Name of Meet
Location of Meet
Level Competing Today
My Teammates Today

My Coach Today
How am I going to relax today?

Am I ready to focus?

Main Goal for Meet

Event & Score Goals for Today
Beam
Bars
Floor
Vault
All Around

Scores Today
Vault   Bars   Beam   Floor   AA

Did I meet my score goals?
What mistakes did I make today?

Will I do anything differently next meet?

GymnasticsBooks.com   © 2013 Goeller

Gymnastics Journal: My Scores, My Goals, My Dreams

Main Goal for Next Meet
_____
_____
_____

Event & Score Goals for Next Meet
Beam _____
Bars _____
Floor _____
Vault _____
All Around _____

One Month Goals
_____
_____
_____

End of Season Goals
_____
_____

One Year Goals
_____
_____
_____
_____
_____

My Dreams
_____
_____
_____
_____

My Thoughts
_____
_____
_____
_____

GymnasticsBooks.com © 2013 Goeller

Gymnastics Journal: My Scores, My Goals, My Dreams

Gymnastics Journal: My Scores, My Goals, My Dreams

Gymnastics Journal: My Scores, My Goals, My Dreams

Date of Meet
Name of Meet
Location of Meet
Level Competing Today
My Teammates Today

My Coach Today
How am I going to relax today?

Am I ready to focus?

Main Goal for Meet

Event & Score Goals for Today
Beam
Bars
Floor
Vault
All Around

Scores Today

Vault	Bars	Beam	Floor	AA

Did I meet my score goals?
What mistakes did I make today?

Will I do anything differently next meet?

GymnasticsBooks.com   © 2013 Goeller

Gymnastics Journal: My Scores, My Goals, My Dreams

Main Goal for Next Meet
_____
_____

Event & Score Goals for Next Meet
Beam _____
Bars _____
Floor _____
Vault _____
All Around _____

One Month Goals
_____
_____
_____

End of Season Goals
_____
_____

One Year Goals
_____
_____
_____
_____
_____

My Dreams
_____
_____
_____
_____

My Thoughts
_____
_____
_____
_____

GymnasticsBooks.com © 2013 Goeller

Gymnastics Journal: My Scores, My Goals, My Dreams

Gymnastics Journal: My Scores, My Goals, My Dreams

Gymnastics Journal: My Scores, My Goals, My Dreams

Date of Meet _____
Name of Meet _____
Location of Meet _____
Level Competing Today _____
My Teammates Today _____
_____
_____

My Coach Today _____
How am I going to relax today? _____
_____

Am I ready to focus? _____
_____

Main Goal for Meet _____
_____
_____

Event & Score Goals for Today
Beam _____
Bars _____
Floor _____
Vault _____
All Around _____

Scores Today

Vault	Bars	Beam	Floor	AA

Did I meet my score goals? _____
What mistakes did I make today? _____
_____

Will I do anything differently next meet? _____
_____

GymnasticsBooks.com © 2013 Goeller

Gymnastics Journal: My Scores, My Goals, My Dreams

Main Goal for Next Meet
_____
_____

Event & Score Goals for Next Meet
Beam _____
Bars _____
Floor _____
Vault _____
All Around _____

One Month Goals
_____
_____

End of Season Goals
_____
_____

One Year Goals
_____
_____
_____
_____

My Dreams
_____
_____
_____

My Thoughts
_____
_____
_____

GymnasticsBooks.com © 2013 Goeller

Gymnastics Journal: My Scores, My Goals, My Dreams

Gymnastics Journal: My Scores, My Goals, My Dreams

Gymnastics Journal: My Scores, My Goals, My Dreams

Other books by Karen Goeller...

1. "Gymnastics Lessons Learned" 2013
   Stories of how gymnasts learned life lessons.

2. "Sentenced to Life in Bed, but I Escaped" 2011
   Readers will be inspired to accept the challenge.

3. "One Swing Set Workout" 2008
   Sample size book, used for promotional purposes.

4. "Fitness on a Swing Set" 2007
   Exercises using a playground swing.

5. "Swing Set Workouts" 2007
   12 exercise programs using a playground swing.

6. "Fitness on Swing Set & Training Programs" 2007
   Exercises and programs using a playground swing.

7. "Gymnastics Conditioning: Five Workouts" 2007
   Strength training and plyometrics.

8. "Gymnastics Conditioning: Tumbling" 2007
   Strength training and drills for tumbling.

9. "Fitness Journal: Goals, Training, Success" 2006
   Spaces for goals, workouts, meals, and diary writing.

10. "Strength Training Journal" 2006
    Charts for the reader to keep track of progress.

11. "Handstand Drills and Conditioning" 2005, 2007
    Pelvic tilt, handstand shape, strength, body tightness.

12. "Gymnastics Journal: Scores, Goals, Dreams" 2005
    Spaces for competition scores, goals, and diary.

Gymnastics Journal: My Scores, My Goals, My Dreams

13. "Gymnastics Conditioning for Legs & Ankles" 2004
    Leg, ankle, foot strength. Landing and skill technique.

14. "Gymnastics Drills: Walkover & Back Handspring" 2004
    Skill technique, flexibility, and strength.

15. "Over 100 Drills and Conditioning Exercises" 2003
    Running, vault, uneven bars, dance, press handstand.

16. "Frequently Asked Questions About Gymn" 2001
    A guide for the gymnast and parent.

17. "Over 75 Drills and Conditioning Exercises" 2001

For more information on these books visit www.GymnasticsBooks.com.
For gymnastics apparel and gifts visit www.GymnasticsTees.com.

Gymnastics Journal: My Scores, My Goals, My Dreams

Gymnastics Journal: My Scores, My Goals, My Dreams

Printed in Great Britain
by Amazon.co.uk, Ltd.,
Marston Gate.